CYCLING
CORNWALL

Tony Farnell

Tor Mark

Published by Tor Mark,
United Downs Industrial Estate,
St Day, Redruth, Cornwall TR16 5HY

www.tormark.co.uk

Published 2018

ISBN 978 0 85025 445 7

Images © Adobe 2018 & © Tor Mark
Snail's Pace Photograph (page 25) © Snail's Pace Café
Jubilee Pool Photograph (page 30) © Martin Nixon www.nixondesign.com

Printed by St Austell Printing Company,
St Austell Business Park,
Cornwall PL25 4FD

AFETY

Although the majority of roads used are country lanes or B roads and have been selected ecause traffic flow is very low, Cornish lanes can present their own unique problems of hich you should be aware. Most are narrow, single track and winding with high Cornish edges and no verges. Just because you have not seen a car for the previous twenty inutes, does not mean that there isn't one coming around the very next sharp corner, o you need to be prepared to stop if necessary to allow the car to pass safely. This is specially important if you encounter a bend on a steep downhill section where you may e travelling surprisingly fast, and find a vehicle coming in the opposite direction and filling e whole of the available road space. So, keep your speed under control especially if pproaching a bend on a downhill slope. Unavoidably, some of the routes cross main or usy roads. In each case, great care is required, as you may encounter heavy or st-moving traffic. If in doubt, dismount and push your bike across the road.

ICYCLES

is important that your bicycle is well maintained, and in particular, the brakes. If you are iring bicycles from a reputable bike hire company, they should take care of this for you; you are borrowing bikes or using your own, you do need to ensure they are in good orking order. Each route gives an indication of the most suitable type of bike - mountain, ad, hybrid or cyclocross.

UNCTURES

unctures are an inevitable part of cycling, so you should always carry at least two spare ner tubes of the correct type for your bike, and/or a puncture repair kit. You will also need vo or three tyre levers to remove your tyre from the wheel rim and a pump to inflate your eplacement inner tube once it is in place. Remember, if you have a puncture without a epair kit, you may end up pushing your bike a long way! Many towns have bike shops in ase you need emergency assistance with unexpected mechanical problems.

LOTHING

you do not cycle frequently, you may not realise the importance of warm, preferably indproof clothing, in all but the hottest weather conditions. Even on quite a warm day, ycling along at 5, 10, 15 miles per hour can produce a noticeable wind chill factor, and is becomes even more pronounced going downhill because you are going faster but oing less work to produce body heat. Equally, sunscreen is always a good idea.

FACILITIES

Facilities you may require, such as car parking, bike hire, toilets, shops, cafés and public houses, are indicated on each route. Many cafés are open all year, but inevitably some close in the winter months or operate restricted hours or days.

ROUTES

Each route is described by means of an accumulated mileage, a description and illustrated by a profile and a map. You may find it helpful to take the appropriate Ordnance Survey map to supplement your navigation. The 1:50,000 Landranger Series 200, 203 or 204 are particularly good. A bike computer will allow you to keep an accurate check on your progress by comparing your current mileage with the accumulated mileage in the text. There is also an indication of the general nature of the route, together with the suggested suitable bike type and time likely to be taken at different average speeds. The mileage, estimated time and the profile may be used to select a route suitable for your fitness, experience and time available.

NATIONAL CYCLE ROUTES

Sustrans is a national charity dedicated to developing and signposting safe cycling routes nationwide, marked by distinctive blue directional signs. Some of the routes in this book follow sections of national cycle routes and the blue signs can be used to simplify navigation.

PARKING

Car parking is specified at or near the start and finish of each ride by means of a postcode and an Ordnance Survey grid reference. Although some of the car parks are free, others require payment. If you have a long or high vehicle you are advised to check beforehand whether the car park is suitable.

SYMBOLS

 Parking

 Toilets

 Café

Public House

 Shops

 Bike Hire

 Bike Shop

 Danger

 Signpost

INTRODUCTION

The aim of this book is to provide a variety of types of bike rides in west and central Cornwall for everyone. About half of the rides are on traffic free trails, which may appeal more to inexperienced cyclists and family groups, while the remainder are road rides, utilising mainly quiet Cornish lanes, which might be favoured by more confident cyclists, be they enthusiasts or commuters.

Both trail and road rides form a network across Cornwall, visiting towns, villages and places catering for a variety of different interests. Many of the routes have been subdivided so that sections can be completed as self-contained short rides, or added together to build up longer rides. For more ambitious riders, different routes can be joined to extend or make the ride circular. Where the rides are between two points, out and back, the routes are described in both directions, making it easier to use with different start and finish points.

When planning your rides, you need to realise that, although Cornwall is not a mountainous county, it is exceedingly hilly. The hills are not long, but they are frequent, and they can be steep. Fortunately, most of the traffic free trails are based on former railway tracks or along valley bottoms making them flat or very gently undulating. However, a number of the road rides will include at least one serious hill. Wherever possible I have tried to ensure the hill comes at the beginning, when you are freshest.

Wherever you ride, there are a few things to keep in mind if you wish to have stress-free cycling. The Important Information provides a few thoughts on how to make the most of your rides. With all outdoor activities, a few simple words will suffice: be safe, sensible and enjoy!

Tony Farnell

CONTENTS

TRAFFIC FREE TRAILS

1 / **PENROSE** TRAIL

DISTANCE:	**4.8 miles**
TIME:	**60 minutes** (at 5 mph), **30 minutes** (at 10 mph), **20 minutes** (at 15 mph)
SURFACE:	Mixture of tarmac, stone and gravel tracks
TERRAIN:	Flat, with some undulations and a hill entering and leaving Porthleven
BIKE:	Mountain, hybrid, cyclocross
PARKING:	Boating Lake car park, Helston TR13 8SG, Kitto's Field car park, Porthleven TR13 9JA
OPINION:	This is a great trail for beginners and families, with the bulk of the route being traffic free and flat. The route wends its way through the wooded Penrose Estate, along the shores of Loe Pool, past the historic Penrose House, onto the coast at Loe Bar and along the cliffs to Porthleven. Additionally, there are numerous alternative trails in and around the Penrose Estate; a map is available at Penrose House

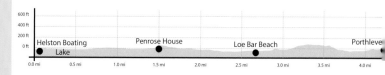

HELSTON - PORTHLEVEN

0.0 mi Start Boating Lake Helston Ⓟ 🚻 ☕ 🚲 🚲 GR SW653270

Cross the bridge over the River Cober on the west side of car park and join the cycle/foot trail

1 1.2 mi Pass gates by lodge house

2 1.4 mi Turn left towards Penrose House

3 1.5 mi Pass Penrose House Ⓟ ☕ GR SW642256

4 2.7 mi Pass the gates by the lodge house (turn left for Loe Bar Beach)

5 3.1 mi Turn right up the gravel track

6 3.3 mi Turn left at the T- junction

7 3.5 mi Turn right onto Coopers Lane

8 3.6 mi Turn left at the junction and proceed downhill

9 3.7 mi At bottom of the hill turn right at the T- junction

10 3.9 mi Turn sharp right up Cliff Road to follow the one-way system, keep left and join Peverell Terrace to pass 🏛, then turn sharp left down Salt Cellar Hill and proceed along the harbour side

4.2 mi Finish Porthleven Harbour Ⓟ 🚻 ☕ 🏛 🛍

GR SW628258

No. on maps

TRAIL 1

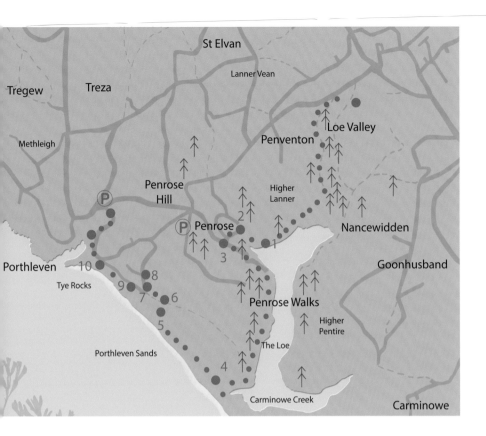

PORTHLEVEN - HELSTON

0.0 mi Start Porthleven Harbour ℗ ᵗᵗ ☕ 🏛 🚪 GR SW628258 Leave along Harbour Road, pass the clock tower and pier, and continue up Cliff Road

10 0.3 mi Fork right along Loe Bar Road

9 0.5 mi Turn left up the the unnamed lane

8 0.6 mi Turn right onto Coopers Lane at the T- junction

7 0.7 mi Turn left through the gate onto a gravel track

6 0.9 mi Turn right and descend the gravel track to cliff top

5 1.1 mi Turn left and follow the track along cliff top

4 1.5 mi Pass gates by the lodge house (or fork right for Loe Bar Beach)

3 2.7 mi Pass Penrose House ℗ ☕ GR SW642256

2 2.8 mi Turn right at the T- junction

1 3.0 mi Pass the gates and lodge house

4.2 mi Finish Boating Lake Helston ℗ ᵗᵗ ☕ 🚲 🚲 GR SW653270

2 / **GREAT FLAT LODE** TRAIL

DISTANCE: **7.5 miles**

TIME: **1 hour 30 minutes** (at 5 mph), **45 minutes** (at 10 mph), **30 minutes** (at 15 mph)

SURFACE: Mixture of tarmac, gravel and stony tracks

TERRAIN: Flat and undulating with one big ascent and descent

BIKE: Mountain, cyclocross

PARKING: Heartlands car park, Pool TR15 3QY

OPINION: This is quite a challenging route in places, with some steep ups and downs and some stretches of rough track. However, the views across St Ives Bay from the top are worth the effort. Near Carnkie you can join the Mineral Trail to link up to the Devoran - Portreath Mineral Tramway (see page 14). There is an alternative start and finish point car park at GR SW683395 TR16 6JS, which would allow you to miss out the busy urban section immediately around Heartlands.

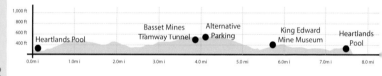

No. on maps

CLOCKWISE ROUTE

0.0 mi Start Heartlands Pool ℗ 👫 ☕ GR SW667411 (clockwise route) Turn right onto Station Road

1 0.1 mi Straight on at the mini roundabout

2 0.2 mi Turn right at the T- junction

3 0.2 mi Turn left at the traffic lights, cross the railway bridge and follow the road around the left bend

4 0.3 mi Cycle straight on when the road bends right (🪧 Great Flat Lode), then fork right up Chapel Hill where the road becomes a rough track, before taking the tarmac cycle trail

5 1.4 mi Fork right up the stony track

6 1.9 mi Turn left at the track crossroads and descend to the road

7 2.0 mi Turn left down the road

8 2.3 mi Turn sharp right up the rough track (🪧 Great Flat Lode) to a road

9 2.9 mi At the T- junction with road cycle straight across into Copper Lane

10 3.0 mi Turn right up the rough track (⊤ Great Flat Lode)

11 3.9 mi Fork left and pass through Basset Mines Tramway Tunnel

12 4.0 mi Cycle straight across the lane following the track around the car park ℗ GR SW683395 TR16 6JS

13 4.1 mi Turn right to pass through the ruined mine buildings

14 4.5 mi Turn left at the road junction into Treskillard and cycle straight on at the crossroads onto a rough track

15 4.6 mi Fork right before Lower Grillis Farm

16 5.0 mi Turn left at the T- junction onto the road

17 5.1 mi Cycle straight on up the rough track as road bends left

18 5.4 mi Turn right down the rough track

19 5.6 mi Cross the road ⚠ onto the track passing King Edward Mine Museum on your right

20 6.0 mi Turn left at the T- junction with the road and then turn immediately right

21 6.1 mi Fork right at the Carn Entral sign, STEEP DESCENT to road ⚠

22 6.5 mi Cycle straight across road ⚠, across the bridge before turning left and following road/track

23 7.0 mi Cycle straight across at the road ⚠ onto track (⊤ Great Flat Lode)

24 7.1 mi Turn right before the old bridge over the railway

25 7.2 mi Turn left at the road

26 7.2 mi Turn left onto the track (⊤ Great Flat Lode), and at the T- junction with the road, turn left ⚠ over the railway bridge

3 7.3 mi At the traffic lights turn right

2 7.3 mi Turn left into Station Road

1 7.4 mi Cycle straight on at the mini roundabout and turn left into Heartlands

7.5 mi Finish Heartlands Pool ℗ ♦♦ ☕ GR SW667411

CARNKIE

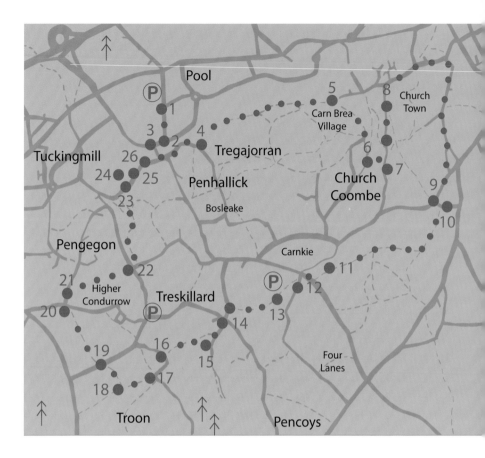

ANTI-CLOCKWISE ROUTE

0.0 mi Start Heartlands Pool Ⓟ 🚻 ☕ GR SW667411 (anti-clockwise route)
Turn right onto Station Road

1   0.1 mi Cycle straight on at the mini roundabout

2   0.2 mi Turn right at the T- junction

3   0.2 mi Turn left at traffic lights, cross railway bridge and turn immediately right along track (⊤ Great Flat Lode)

26   0.4 mi Join the road ⚠

25   0.4 mi Turn right onto the track (⊤ Great Flat Lode)

24   0.5 mi Turn left at the old bridge crossing the railway

23   0.6 mi Cycle straight across the road ⚠ through the gate and onto a gravel track which eventually becomes tarmac

22   1.2 mi Cross the stream and road ⚠ and climb a very steep tarmac path

21   1.6 mi At the track junction keep left

20 1.7 mi Turn left onto the road, then immediately right onto a track (⸸ Great Flat Lode) to pass King Edward Mine Museum on your left

19 2.1 mi Cross the road ⚠ onto a track (⸸ Great Flat Lode)

18 2.3 mi At the track T- junction, take the left-hand route

17 2.6 mi Join the road and continue straight on

16 2.7 mi Turn right onto the track (⸸ Great Flat Lode)

15 3.1 mi Join the road and proceed through Treskillard

14 3.2 mi Turn right up the track (⸸ Great Flat Lode)

13 3.3 mi Pass through the ruined mine buildings and turn left

12 3.6 mi Turn left after passing between old mine buildings, follow the track around the car park ℗ GR SW683395 TR16 6JS and cross a lane

11 3.8 mi Pass through Basset Mines Tramway Tunnel and cross the lane

10 4.8 mi Turn left onto Copper Lane

9 4.9 mi At road junction cycle straight across onto the track (⸸ Great Flat Lode)

8 5.5 mi At junction with road turn sharp left

7 5.8 mi Turn sharp right onto the track (⸸ Great Flat Lode)

6 5.9 mi At track crossing turn right

5 6.4 mi At junction with tarmac cycle trail turn left and continue until it be comes a rough track, then a road, keep right and proceed downhill

4 7.2 mi At junction with road turn right ⚠ take care and follow road over railway bridge

3 7.3 mi At traffic lights turn right

2 7.3 mi Turn left into Station Road

1 7.4 mi Straight on at mini roundabout and turn left into Heartlands

    7.5 mi Finish Heartlands Pool ℗ 🚻 ☕ GR SW667411

VIEWS FROM ACROSS ST IVES BAY

3 / **MINERAL TRAMWAY** TRAIL

DISTANCE: **11 miles**

TIME: **2 hours 10 minutes** (at 5 mph), **1 hour 5 minutes** (at 10 mph), **45 minutes** (at 15 mph)

SURFACE: Mixture of mainly gravel and stone tracks with some quiet tarmac lanes and cycle paths

TERRAIN: Flat and gently undulating

BIKE: Mountain, cyclocross, hybrid

PARKING: The Beach car park, Portreath TR16 4NQ, By-pass car park, Devoran TR3 6PG

OPINION: One of my favourite off-road routes. This is an historic purpose-built coast-to-coast trail along an old mineral railway. Most of it is traffic free and gradients are generally gradual. There are numerous refreshment facilities along the way and you can nip in for a swim at Portreath. From Twelveheads you can divert to the Mineral Trail link, which connects you to the Great Flat Lode Trail, (see page 10)

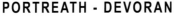

PORTREATH - DEVORAN

0.0 mi Start Portreath GR SW653453 From ⓟ turn left on B3300 Redruth Road and then fork left along Sunnyvale Road

1 0.6 mi Fork left onto Mineral Railway Trail

2 1.1 mi Cross lane ⚠

3 1.9 mi Cross lane ⚠

4 2.3 mi Cross road ⚠ at Cambrose to turn left along tarmac cycle/footpath, passing 🚴 on left

5 2.9 mi Turn right at junction into lane

6 3.1 mi Straight on ⚠ at crossroads

7 3.3 mi Straight on ⚠ at crossroads onto track

8 4.9 mi Turn left up cycle track, then right at T- junction with road onto tarmac cycle/footpath and cross bridge over A30 dual carriageway

14

9 5.1 mi Cross road ⚠ to turn left when cycle path ends, proceed under railway bridge, turn right ⚠ at 🏛 and proceed through car park

10 5.4 mi Cross road ⚠ and turn left onto cycle/footpath

11 5.5 mi Turn right at crossroads, staying on cycle/footpath

12 5.7 mi Cross road ⚠ onto tarmac cycle trail and proceed through Unity Woods

13 6.6 mi Join lane

14 6.7 mi Straight across ⚠ at crossroads

15 6.8 mi Turn right at T- junction down short hill and turn left at bottom and proceed down Poldice Valley

16 8.2 mi Join road at Twelveheads 🍴 GR SW759422 straight on

17 8.4 mi Turn left onto trail

18 9.0 mi At Bissoe 🍴 🚲 🚲 GR 769415 turn right on road ⚠, cross bridge over Carnon River and turn immediately left onto track

19 9.5 mi Cross lane ⚠

20 10.1 mi Cross lane ⚠

21 10.7 mi Cross road ⚠

22 11.0 mi After passing under road bridge, turn right to car park

11.1 mi Finish Devoran ℗ 🚻 🏛 GR SW790394

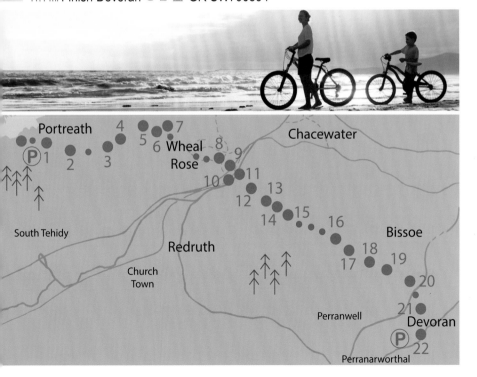

DEVORAN - PORTREATH

0.0 mi Start Devoran ⓟ 🚻 🏛 GR SW790394 Turn left out of ⓟ

22 0.1 mi At T- junction turn left on track to proceed under main road bridge

21 0.5 mi Cross road ⚠

20 1.1 mi Cross lane ⚠

19 1.7 mi Cross lane ⚠

18 2.2 mi At Bissoe ☕ 🚲 🚲 GR 769415 turn right on road ⚠, cross bridge over Carnon River and turn immediately left onto track

17 2.8 mi Turn right onto lane

16 3.0 mi Straight on taking track as lane bends to the right at Twelveheads ☕ GR SW759422 climbing gradually up Poldice Valley

15 4.4 mi Turn right at T- junction, up short hill, and then turn left onto lane

14 4.6 mi Straight across ⚠ at crossroads

13 4.7 mi Fork left onto track and proceed through Unity Woods

12 5.5 mi Cross B3298 ⚠ and follow cycle/footpath

11 5.7 mi Turn left at crossroads and stay on cycle/footpath

10 5.8 mi Cross road ⚠ at cycle crossing into 🏛 car park. Proceed through car park and turn left onto road ⚠

9 6.0 mi At T- junction cross road ⚠ and turn right on cycle/footpath and cross bridge over A30 dual carriageway

8 6.2 mi Turn left onto cycle track, and then turn right at bottom of slope

7 7.8 mi Straight on ⚠ at crossroads onto lane

6 8.0 mi Straight on ⚠ at crossroads

5 8.2 mi Turn left at T- junction onto cycle/footpath passing 🚲 on right

4 8.8 mi Cross road ⚠ at Cambrose to turn right, then immediately fork left along track

3 9.2 mi Cross lane ⚠

2 10.0 mi Cross lane ⚠

1 10.5 mi Turn right into Sunnyvale Road, then right again onto B3300

11.1 mi Finish Portreath ⓟ 🚻 ☕ 🚲 🚻 🏛 GR SW653453

PORTREATH

4 / **PENTEWAN** TRAIL

DISTANCE: **3.8 miles**

TIME: **43 minutes** (at 5 mph), **22 minutes** (at 10 mph), **14 minutes** (at 15 mph)

SURFACE: Mixture of tarmac, gravel and earth road, track and path, muddy in places after rain

TERRAIN: Downhill out of St Austell, then flat

BIKE: Mountain, hybrid, cyclocross

PARKING: Priory Road car park, St Austell PL25 5AB, Pentewan car park, Pentewan PL26 6BX

OPINION: This is a great introductory ride for beginners or novices which is well signposted. It's flat and traffic free, apart from the uphill drag into St Austell, but you can always miss this bit out if you don't feel like it! There are refreshment alternatives at Pentewan and a beach if you fancy a swim.

ST AUSTELL – PENTEWAN

0.0 mi Start St Austell ⓟ ᵗᶦ ☕ 🛍 🏛 GR SX013524 Join cycle/footpath at junction of Sawles Road and B3273

1 0.4 mi Fork left onto lane at sewage works

2 0.6 mi At end of lane, fork right onto tarmac cycle/footpath

3 1.1 mi At junction, turn left onto lane, then right onto track

4 1.4 mi Turn right into lane and left onto track

5 1.7 mi Fork right just before gate into Peckhill Wood and follow St Austell River downstream.

6 2.3 mi Pass ⓟ on right

7 2.6 mi At bridge, straight on (turn right over bridge for Lost Gardens of Heligan and Mevagissey)

8 2.8 mi Fork left into woods

9 3.6 mi Just past 🚲 turn left at T- junction onto West End road and proceed into Pentewan

3.8 mi Finish Pentewan ⓟ ᵗᶦ ☕ 🛍 🚲 🏛 GR SX017472

PENTEWAN – ST AUSTELL

0.0 mi Start Pentewan ⓟ 🚻 ☕ 🛄 🚲 🏛 GR SX017472 Take West End road out of centre

9 0.2 mi Turn right at 🚲 onto trail

8 1.0 mi Join track and follow St Austell River upstream

7 1.2 mi At bridge, cycle straight on (turn left over bridge for Lost Gardens of Heligan and Mevagissey)

6 1.5 mi Pass ⓟ on left

5 2.1 mi At track junction turn left

4 2.4 mi Turn right into lane followed by left onto track

3 2.7 mi At junction, turn left onto lane, then right onto tarmac cycle/footpath

2 3.2 mi Leave cycle/footpath and bear left onto lane

1 3.4 mi Turn right just past sewage works onto cycle/footpath next to B3273 towards St Austell

3.8 mi Finish St Austell ⓟ 🚻 ☕ 🛄 🏛 GR SX013524

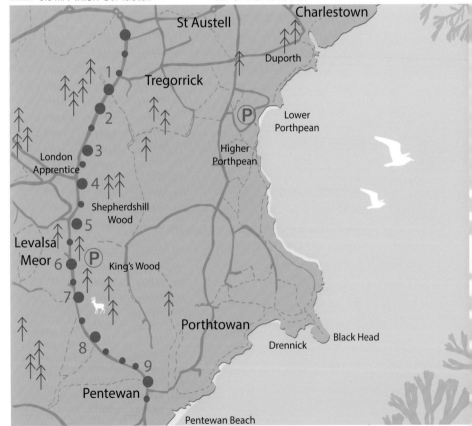

5 / **COAST AND CLAY** TRAIL

DISTANCE: **12 miles**

TIME: **2 hours 30 minutes** (at 5 mph), **1 hour 15 minutes** (at 10 mph), **48 minutes** (at 15 mph)

SURFACE: Mixture of tarmac and gravel road, track and path, muddy in places after wet weather

TERRAIN: Very steep hill out of Mevagissey and long steady climb through St Austell and clay hills

BIKE: Mountain, hybrid, cyclocross

PARKING: River Street car park, Mevagissey PL26 6EU, Eden Project car park, Bodelva PL24 2SG

OPINION: This is a ride of many contrasts, starting at the working fishing port of Mevagissey and finishing at the spectacular domes of the Eden Project. In between you have some steep hills, a flat valley ride on the Pentewan Trail, a traverse of St Austell town centre and a climb up the summits of the historic clay hills with spectacular views across moors and coast.

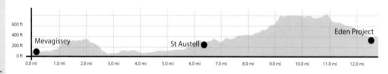

MEVAGISSEY – EDEN PROJECT

0.0 mi Start Mevagissey ℗ ♟♟ ☕ 🛍 🏛 GR SX014448 Leave in St Austell direction on B3273 River Street

1 0.3 mi Fork left onto track to pass Sports Centre and follow track up steep hill (⚠ - **BEWARE** bikes coming fast downhill)

2 1.9 mi At T- junction turn right under bridge (or turn left for The Lost Gardens of Heligan) and follow track downhill and then parallel to B3273

3 3.0 mi Cross B3273 ⚠, follow cycle/footpath beside road, then turn right to cross St Austell River bridge

4 3.2 mi Turn left and follow Pentewan Trail signs towards St Austell

5 5.0 mi After passing sewage works on left, turn right onto cycle/footpath alongside B3273

6 5.4 mi At St Austell 30mph signs, turn right into Sawles Road

TRAIL 5

7 5.7 mi At T- junction turn left up Sawles Road

8 5.8 mi At traffic lights straight on to continue uphill on Sawles Road

9 6.0 mi Turn left into Eastbourne Road

10 6.2 mi At traffic lights, straight across onto bike path and East Hill

11 6.3 mi St Austell Church Street Ⓟ ♦♦ 🚲 ☕ 🛈 🏛 GR SX013524 Continue around the church into Market Street, then turn left up Market Hill and continue uphill on North Street

12 6.4 mi After crossing railway bridge, turn left into Tremena Road

13 6.6 mi As Tremena Road bends right, turn left onto cycle path

14 8.0 mi At junction straight on ⊤ Clay Trails Eden Project (turn sharp left to visit Wheal Martyn Clay Mining Museum) and continue climbing, following signs for Clay Trails Eden Project

15 9.0 mi Cross bridge over A391 and follow signs to Clay Trails Eden Project through former clay pits, then descending

12.0 mi Finish Eden Project Ⓟ ♦♦ ☕ GR SX048547

EDEN PROJECT – MEVAGISSEY

0.0 mi Start Eden Project Ⓟ ♦♦ ☕ GR SX048547 From bike park follow signs Clay Trails St Austell mainly climbing uphill

15 3.0 mi Cross bridge over A391 and continue following signs for Clay Trails St Austell

14 4.0 mi At track junction fork left ⊤ Clay Trails St Austell (fork right to visit Wheal Martyn Clay Mining Museum) and follow track downhill

13 5.4 mi Join Tremena Road

12 5.6 mi At junction turn right, cross railway bridge and proceed down North Street, turn left, down Market Hill, at bottom turn right into Market Street, and follow road around church into Church Street

11 5.8 mi St Austell Church Street Ⓟ ♦♦ 🚲 ☕ 🛈 🏛 GR SX013524 Turn right along East Hill and onto bike path

10 6.0 mi At traffic lights, straight across into Eastbourne Road

9 6.2 mi At junction keep right into Sawles Road and proceed downhill

8 6.4 mi At traffic lights straight on to continue downhill on Sawles Road

7 6.5 mi At bottom of hill turn right

6 6.8 mi At T- junction, turn left onto bike/footpath alongside B3273

5 7.2 mi Fork left at sewage works and follow Pentewan Trail signs towards Pentewan

4 9.0 mi Turn right to cross bridge over St Austell River (⊤ Mevagissey and Heligan),

then turn left onto cycle/footpath, alongside B3273

3 9.1 mi Cross road ⚠ and take cycle/footpath (☂ Mevagissey/Heligan) proceeding uphill

2 10.2 mi At top of hill pass under bridge and turn left ☂ Mevagissey (or straight on for The Lost Gardens of Heligan) and follow track down steep hill (⚠ - control your speed)

1 11.7 mi Pass Sports Centre on right and join River Street ⚠ into town

12.0 mi Finish Mevagissey Ⓟ 🛉 ☕ 🛍 🏛 GR SX014448

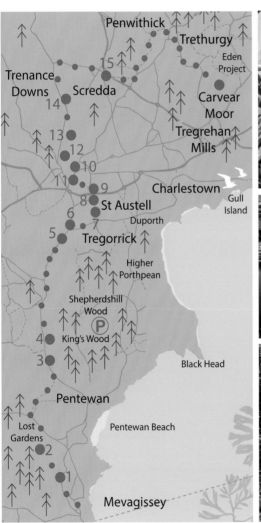

EDEN PROJECT

MEVAGISSEY HARBOUR

THE LOST GARDENS OF HELIGAN

6 / CAMEL TRAIL

DISTANCE: **12.8 miles**

TIME: **3 hours** (at 5 mph), **1 hour 30 minutes** (at 10 mph), **50 minutes** (at 15 mph)

SURFACE: Mixture of tarmac and gravel track

TERRAIN: Flat apart from steady climb from Dunmere to Bodmin and gentle climb from Dunmere to Wenfordbridge

BIKE: Mountain, hybrid, cyclocross, road

PARKING: Link Road car park, Padstow PL28 8AY, Fore Street car park, Bodmin PL31 2DB

OPINION: Without a doubt this is the best cycle trail in Cornwall. It is purpose-built with numerous refreshment opportunities, and flat apart from the grind uphill from Dunmere to Bodmin centre, but you don't have to do this bit if you don't like hills! You can follow National Cycle Route 3 through Bodmin to Lanhydrock House and Gardens, where there are several off-road trails.

PADSTOW - BODMIN

No. on maps

0.0 mi Start Padstow Ⓟ ♦♦ 🍴 🛒 🚲 🚲 GR SW919751 Leave along Riverside passing National Lobster Hatchery and join Camel Trail

1 1.0 mi Cross bridge over Little Petherick Creek

2 2.0 mi Cross Oldtown Cove

3 2.6 mi Cross Pinkson Creek

4 5.2 mi Pass under Wadebridge by-pass viaduct

5 5.7 mi Wadebridge Ⓟ ♦♦ 🍴 🛒 🚲 🚲 GR SW990724

6 7.2 mi Cycle past Shooting Range Platform

7 9.0 mi Cycle past Grogley Halt

8 9.8 mi Cycle past Camel Valley Vineyard

9 10.4 mi Cycle past Nanstallon Halt 🍴

10 10.8 mi Cycle past Boscarne Junction

11 11.1 mi Cycle past Dunmere Halt

12 11.2 mi Dunmere Ⓟ ♦♦ 🏛 GR SX047676 Follow trail uphill (☇ Bodmin)

TRAIL 6

13 11.3 mi At fork straight on (or sharp left for Wenfordbridge)

14 12.3 mi Join Scarletts Well Road, pass Bodmin Jail and proceed along Berrycoombe Road and Pool Street

12.8 mi Finish Bodmin Ⓟ 👥 ☕ 🍴 🚲 🚲 GR SX072671

BODMIN – PADSTOW

0.0 mi Start Bodmin Ⓟ 👥 ☕ 🍴 🚲 🚲 GR SX072671 Leave along Pool Street, Berrycoombe Road and Scarlett's Well Road, passing Bodmin Jail

14 0.5 mi Fork left to join trail and proceed downhill

13 1.5 mi At fork straight on (or right for Wenfordbridge)

12 1.6 mi Dunmere Ⓟ 👥 🏛 GR SX047676

11 1.7 mi Cycle past Dunmere Halt

10 2.0 mi Cycle past Boscarne Junction

9 2.4 mi Cycle past Nanstallon Halt ☕

8 3.0 mi Cycle past Camel Valley Vineyard

7 3.8 mi Cycle past Grogley Halt

6 5.6 mi Cycle past Shooting Range Platform

5 7.1 mi Wadebridge Ⓟ 👥 ☕ 🍴 🚲 🚲 GR SW990724

4 7.6 mi Pass under Wadebridge by-pass viaduct

3 10.2 mi Cross Pinkson Creek

2 10.8 mi Cross Oldtown Cove

1 11.8 mi Cross bridge over Little Petherick Creek

12.8 mi Finish Padstow Ⓟ 👥 ☕ 🍴 🚲 🚲 GR SW919751

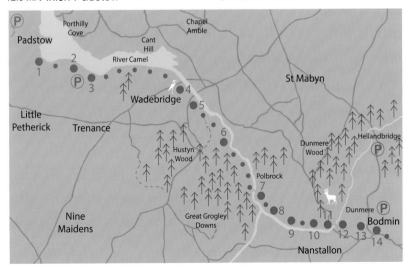

7 / **DUNMERE** TRAIL

DISTANCE: **6.8 miles**

TIME: **1 hour 20 minutes** (at 5 mph), **45 minutes** (at 10 mph), **25 minutes** (at 15 mph)

SURFACE: Gravel track

TERRAIN: Almost flat with a very gradual rise from Dunmere to Wenfordbridge

BIKE: Mountain, hybrid, cyclocross, road

PARKING: Borough Arms car park, Dunmere PL31 2RD, Snail's Pace Café car park, Wenfordbridge PL30 3PN

OPINION: This is a delightful wooded and rural valley route, following the river. Refreshment is available all the year at Dunmere and seasonally at Wenfordbridge.

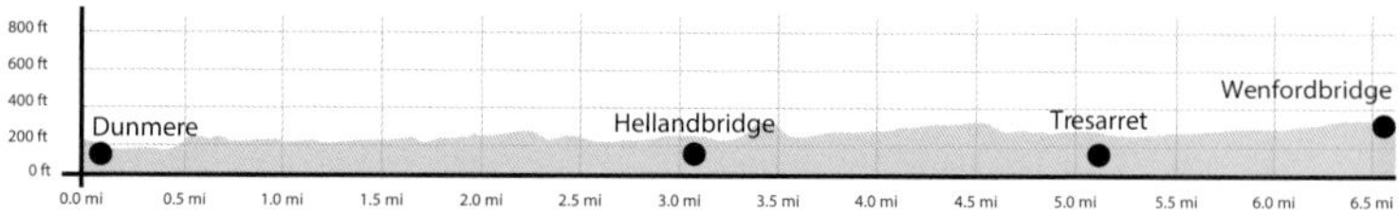

No. on maps

DUNMERE - WENFORDBRIDGE

0.0 mi Start Dunmere Ⓟ 🚻 🏛 GR SX046675

1 0.2 mi Follow trail uphill towards Bodmin and turn sharp left (Wenfordbridge)

2 3.2 mi Straight across road ⚠ at Hellandbridge

3 5.3 mi Straight across road ⚠ at Tresarrett

4 6.2 mi Straight across road ⚠ and pass disused factory

6.8 mi Finish Wenfordbridge Ⓟ 🚻 ☕ 🚲 GR SX085751

WENFORDBRIDGE - DUNMERE

0.0 mi Start Wenfordbridge Ⓟ 🚻 ☕ 🚲 GR SX085751

4 0.6 mi After passing disused factory, straight across road ⚠

3 1.5 mi Straight across road ⚠ at Tresarrett

2 3.6 mi Straight across road ⚠ at Hellandbridge

1 6.6 mi At junction turn sharp right (Wadebridge)

6.8 mi Finish Dunmere Ⓟ 🚻 🏛 GR SX046675

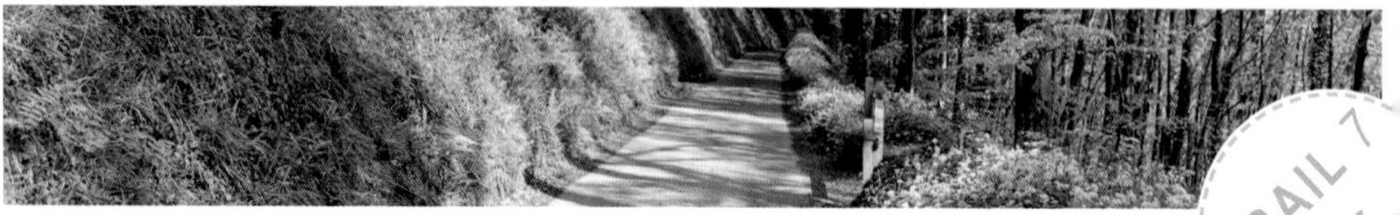

Wenfordbridge

Cross
Hill

Penpont

4

Camel
Trail

Longstone

3

Heligan
Wood

Coldrinnick
Woods

Hellandbridge

2

Helland

Pencarrow
Wood

Racecourse
Downs

Helland
Wood

Outlands
Wood

Dunmere
Wood

Callywith

Dunmere

1

Bodmin

TRAFFIC FREE TRAILS (GREEN)

1 / **PENROSE TRAIL** (4.8 MILES) FLAT / UNDULATING
2 / **GREAT FLAT LODE TRAIL** (7.5 MILES) UNDULATING / HILLY
3 / **MINERAL TRAMWAY TRAIL** (11 MILES) FLAT / UNDULATING
4 / **PENTEWAN TRAIL** (3.8 MILES) FLAT
5 / **COAST AND CLAY TRAIL** (8 MILES) HILLY
6 / **CAMEL TRAIL – PADSTOW** (12.8 MILES) FLAT
7 / **DUNMERE TRAIL** (6.8 MILES) FLAT

ROAD RIDES (BLUE)

8 / **HAYLE – MOUSEHOLE** (12 MILES) FLAT
9 / **MARAZION – PORTHLEVEN** (10 MILES) UNDULATING
10 / **HELSTON – FALMOUTH** (12 MILES) HILLY
11 / **FALMOUTH – TRURO** (18 MILES) HILLY
12 / **ST AUSTELL – BODMIN** (14 MILES) HILLY
13 / **PERRANPORTH – PORTREATH** (12 MILES) UNDULATING
14 / **PORTREATH – HAYLE** (10 MILES) UNDULATING

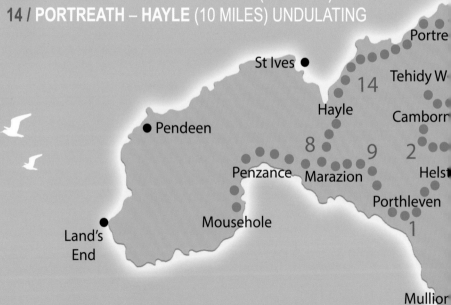

ROAD RIDES

8 / **HAYLE** - MOUSEHOLE

DISTANCE:	**12 miles**
TIME:	**3 hours** (at 5 mph), **1 hour 30 minutes** (at 10 mph), **50 minutes** (at 15 mph)
SURFACE:	Mainly tarmac lanes with cycle/footpath between Longrock and Penzance
TERRAIN:	Mainly flat with one or two small undulations
BIKE:	Mountain, hybrid, cyclocross, road
PARKING:	The Parade car park, Mousehole TR196PR, Foundry Square car park, Hayle TR27 4HQ
OPINION:	Much of this route is flat and some of it is traffic free, particularly between Long Rock and Penzance, making it ideal for inexperienced riders. There are fantastic views across Mount's Bay, numerous towns and villages with pubs, cafés and restaurants in abundance and a great beach if you fancy a swim. The route uses the Sustrans National Cycle Route 3, so you can follow the distinctive blue signs instead of following the instructions below.

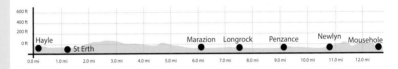

HAYLE - MOUSEHOLE

No. on maps

0.0 mi Start Hayle Foundry Square Ⓟ †♦ ☕ ⛻ 🚲 🏛 GR SW558371
Leave on Penzance road underneath railway viaduct and join cycle/footpath on left

1 0.7 mi Join Chenhalls Road ⚠ with care

2 1.7 mi In St Erth Ⓟ ⛻ 🏛 GR SW549350 keep right over bridge

3 4.3 mi At T- junction turn left and proceed through Gwallon

4 4.7 mi After passing under bridge turn right onto cycle/footpath

5 5.0 mi At end of cycle path join New Dairy Lane and Green Lane West

6 5.5 mi Join Green Lane

7 5.7 mi Fork right (or fork left to visit Marazion, Ⓟ †♦ ☕ ⛻ 🏛 GR SW517306) and then keep right onto main road ⚠

8 5.8 mi Join cycle/footpath on left

9 6.6 mi Longrock Ⓟ †♦ ☕ ⛻ 🏛 GR SW500314
Follow tarmac/gravel cycle/footpath along coast

ROAD 8

10 8.2 mi Penzance Harbour ⓟ ♛ ☕ ⓗ 🚲 🏛 GR SW476305
Follow cycle trail through car park

11 8.3 mi At car park exit turn left ⚠ with care, pass Jubilee Pool, Cornwall's unique Art Deco open air swimming pool on left and proceed along promenade

12 9.7 mi Newlyn ⓟ ♛ ☕ ⓗ 🏛 GR SW462290 Proceed through Newlyn past the fish market and harbour on the left

13 11.2 mi Pass Penlee Lifeboat Station on left
11.8 mi Finish Mousehole Harbour ⓟ ♛ ☕ ⓗ 🏛 GR SW469264

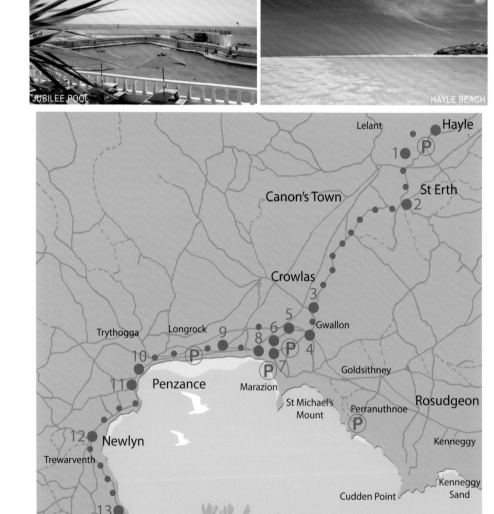

JUBILEE POOL

HAYLE BEACH

MOUSEHOLE HARBOUR

MOUSEHOLE - HAYLE

0.0 mi Start Mousehole Harbour ⓟ ♦♦ ☕ 🛈 🏛 GR SW469264 Proceed east along main road in Penzance direction

13 0.6 mi Pass Penlee Lifeboat Station on right

12 2.1 mi Follow the one-way system into Newlyn ⓟ ♦♦ ☕ 🛈 🏛 GR SW462290 passing the fish market and harbour on the right, in centre keep right over bridge and proceed to Penzance, joining the promenade and continue past the Jubilee Pool, Cornwall's unique Art Deco open air swimming pool on right

11 3.5 mi Cross bridge, turn right ⚠ into Penzance harbour car park and follow cycle track through car park

10 3.6 mi Penzance Harbour ⓟ ♦♦ ☕ 🛈 🚴 🏛 GR SW476305 Leave along tarmac/gravel cycle/footpath following coast

9 5.2 mi Longrock ⓟ ♦♦ ☕ 🛈 🏛 GR SW500314

8 6.0 mi When cycle/footpath finishes join main road ⚠

7 6.1 mi Fork left into Green Lane (or straight on to visit Marazion ⓟ ♦♦ ☕ 🛈 🏛 GR SW517306) and then keep left at T- junction into Green Lane

6 6.3 mi Fork left into Green Lane West and New Dairy Lane

5 6.8 mi At end of lane keep left onto cycle/footpath

4 7.1 mi At T- junction with lane turn left ⚠ under bridge and proceed through Gwallon

3 7.5 mi Turn right (ꝉ St Erth)

2 10.1 mi In St Erth ⓟ 🛈 🏛 GR SW549350 Cross bridge and keep left along Chenhalls Road

1 11.1 mi Cross road ⚠ onto cycle/footpath, then join main road ⚠ into Hayle and pass under railway viaduct

11.8 mi Finish Hayle Foundry Square ⓟ ♦♦ ☕ 🛈 🚴 🏛 GR SW558371

9 / **MARAZION** - PORTHLEVEN

DISTANCE: **10 miles**

TIME: **2 hours** (at 5 mph), **1 hour** (at 10 mph), **45 minutes** (at 15 mph)

SURFACE: Tarmac lanes

TERRAIN: Undulating

BIKE: Mountain, hybrid, cyclocross, road

PARKING: Folly Field car park, Marazion TR17 0EZ, Kitto's Field car park, Porthleven TR13 9JA

OPINION: This is an interesting rural route along typical Cornish lanes linking Marazion and its iconic St Michael's Mount with the thriving fishing harbour area of Porthleven. On the way, a short diversion would allow you to scramble down the cliff path to the little known Rinsey Beach.

MARAZION - PORTHLEVEN

0.0 mi Start Marazion ⓟ ᵗⁱ̈ ☕ 🛍 🏛 GR SW517306

Leave along Fore Street in direction of Helston

1 0.4 mi Turn left up Shop Hill (⌖ Surgery), then immediately turn right (⌖ Plain-an-Gwarry)

2 2.1 mi At T- junction turn right

3 2.6 mi At crossroads turn left onto B3280 (⌖ Redruth)

4 2.9 mi Turn right (⌖ Prussia Cove)

5 3.5 mi At T- junction turn left (⌖ Prussia Cove)

6 4.7 mi At T- junction turn right uphill

7 6.1 mi At T- junction turn right (⌖ Ashton)

8 7.7 mi At T- junction in Ashton 🏛 turn left ⚠ with care onto A394, then turn immediately right (⌖ Rinsey)

9 8.1 mi Keep left (straight on for Rinsey Beach)

10.7 mi Finish Porthleven ⓟ ᵗⁱ̈ ☕ 🛍 🏛 GR SW628258

CAUSEWAY TOWARDS ST MICHAEL'S MOUNT

ROAD 9

PORTHLEVEN - MARAZION

0.0 mi Start Porthleven ℗ 🚻 ☕ 🏧 🏛 GR SW628258 Proceed west along Harbour Head and turn left up Beacon Road

9 2.6 mi At Rinsey keep sharp right (turn left for Rinsey Beach)

8 3.0 mi At T- junction in Ashton 🏛 GR SW603285 turn left ⚠ with care onto A394, then turn immediately right (⳨ Godolphin Cross)

7 4.6 mi Turn left (⳨ Millpool)

6 6.0 mi Turn left (⳨ Millpool)

5 7.2 mi Turn right (⳨ St Erth)

4 7.8 mi At T- junction turn left ⚠ onto B3280 (⳨ Penzance)

3 8.1 mi At crossroads turn right ⚠ (⳨ St Erth)

2 8.6 mi Turn left and proceed through Plain-an-Gwarry

1 10.3 mi On entering Marazion turn left at T- junction down Shop Hill and immediately right into Fore Street

10.7 mi Finish Marazion ℗ 🚻 ☕ 🏧 🏛 GR SW517306

RINSEY HEAD

PORTHLEVEN

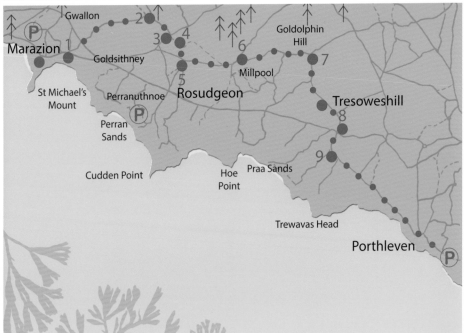

10 / **HELSTON** - FALMOUTH

DISTANCE: **12 miles**

TIME: **2 hours 36 minutes** (at 5 mph), **1 hour 18 minutes** (at 10 mph), **50 minutes** (at 15 mph)

SURFACE: Tarmac lanes and B roads

TERRAIN: Hilly

BIKE: Mountain, hybrid, cyclocross, road

PARKING: Town Quarry car park, Falmouth TR11 3BX, Tyacke Road car park, Helston TR13 8RY

OPINION: This route takes you through some delightful Cornish countryside, but has numerous steep climbs and descents. There are refreshments at Trewardreva Mill and Gweek, where a short diversion would allow you to visit the Seal Sanctuary.

FALMOUTH - HELSTON

No. on maps

0.0 mi Start The Moor, Falmouth Ⓟ 👬 ☕ 🏧 🏛 🚲 GR SW80632
From roundabout follow one way system into Killigrew Street, take first right into Brook Street and left into Berkeley Vale and Kimberley Park Road

1 0.6 mi Straight on at traffic lights

2 1.5 mi Straight on at roundabout (🕆 Mawnan Smith) into Kergilliack Roa

3 1.7 mi Turn left at T- junction (🕆 Mawnan Smith). Proceed through Lamanva, Treverva, Trewardreva Mill ☕ and Brill

4 7.9 mi Gweek 🏛 🏧 GR SW706268 Follow the signs if you wish to visit the Seal Sanctuary or immediately after crossing bridge, turn right uphill (🕆 Redruth)

5 8.0 mi Turn left (🕆 Pemboa)

6 11.1 mi At mini roundabout turn right (🕆 Outbound traffic)

7 11.3 mi At T- junction turn right ⚠ onto A394 and join cycle/footpath

8 11.6 mi At roundabout straight on

9 11.8 mi At traffic lights turn left into Trengrouse Way and continue to Meneage Street

12.1 mi Finish Meneage Street Helston Ⓟ 🚲 🚲 ☕ 🏧 👬 🏛
GR SW659274

HELSTON - FALMOUTH

0.0 mi Start Meneage Street Helson ℗ 🚴 🚲 ☕ 🛏 🚻 🏛 GR SW659274.

From Meneage Street, proceed up Trengrouse Way

9 0.3 mi Turn right at traffic lights onto A394 (🕇 Falmouth)

8 0.5 mi At roundabout straight on (🕇 Lizard)

7 0.8 mi Turn left (🕇 Pemboa)

6 1.0 mi At mini roundabout turn left (🕇 Recycling centre)

5 3.0 mi At T- junction turn right

4 4.1 mi At T- junction turn left (🕇 Falmouth). Pass through Gweek 🛏 GR SW706268

Straight on (🕇 Falmouth), and proceed through Brill, Trewardreva Mill ☕,
Treverva and Lamanva (or follow the signs if you wish to visit the Seal Sanctuary)

3 10.4 mi Turn right (🕇 Truro) into Kergilliack Road

2 10.6 mi Straight on at roundabout (🕇 Falmouth) into Trescobeas Road

1 11.5 mi Straight on at traffic lights down Kimberley Park Road and past Kimberley
Park on right, into Berkeley Vale and follow one-way system into The Moor

12.1 mi Finish The Moor, Falmouth ℗ 🚻 ☕ 🛏 🏛 🚴 GR SW806329

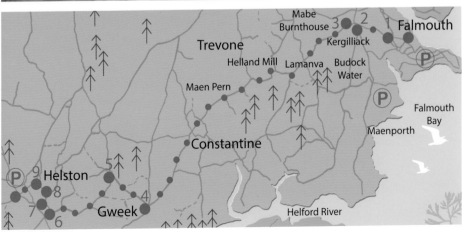

11 / **FALMOUTH** - TRURO

DISTANCE: **18 miles**

TIME: **3 hours 45 minutes** (at 5 mph), **1 hour 50 minutes** (at 10 mph), **1 hour 15 minutes** (at 15 mph)

SURFACE: Tarmac lanes and B roads

TERRAIN: Hilly

BIKE: Mountain, hybrid, cyclocross, road

PARKING: Town Quarry car park, Falmouth TR11 3BX, Lemon Quay car park, Truro TR1 2EH

OPINION: This is quite a tough ride in terms of hills and distance, but it does avoid busy roads, provide a variety of refreshment stops, most notably Argal Reservoir, Stithians village and Bissoe, and links two historic Cornish towns. To avoid the busy urban parts, you can start or finish at Argal, Stithians or Bissoe.

FALMOUTH - TRURO

0.0 mi Start The Moor, Falmouth Ⓟ 🚻 ☕ 🛍 🏛 🚲 GR SW806329
From roundabout follow one-way system into Killigrew Street, take first right into Brook Street and left into Berkeley Vale

1 0.4 mi Straight on at traffic lights

2 1.3 mi Straight on at roundabout (🕇 Mawnan Smith) into Kergilliack Road

3 1.5 mi Turn left at T- junction (🕇 Mawnan Smith)

4 3.0 mi Straight on at crossroads (🕇 Gweek) or turn right for Argal Reservoir Ⓟ ☕ 🚻 GR SW7623287 (🕇 Mabe)

5 4.6 mi Turn right (🕇 Stithians), pass cement works on right at top of hill

6 6.6 mi Turn left at T- junction ⚠ onto main Falmouth - Helston road A39

7 6.7 mi Turn right ⚠ at car repair garage

8 7.2 mi Turn right at T- junction (🕇 Stithians)

9 8.8 mi Turn left at crossroads into Stithians village, Stithians Ⓟ 🛍 ☕ 🚻 GR SW732369

10 9.4 mi Turn right on unsigned road opposite church

11 9.7 mi Cross bridge and turn left

12 11.0 mi Turn right at T- junction († Gwennap)

13 11.3 mi Turn right ⚠ on main Falmouth - Redruth road A393

14 11.4 mi Turn immediately left

15 11.4 mi Straight on at crossroads

16 12.6 mi Turn left at crossroads into Frogpool 🏛

17 13.2 mi Turn right at Cusgarne

18 14.0 mi Cross bridge over Carnon River and turn left into visitor's area Bissoe Cycle Hire Ⓟ 🚲 🚲 ☕ GR SW769415 Turn left out of visitor's area

19 14.6 mi Fork left immediately after crossroads

20 15.9 mi Straight on at crossroads

21 16.2 mi Straight on at crossroads

22 16.9 mi Cross railway bridge and turn right at T- junction

23 18.0 mi Cross dual carriageway A390 Green Lane ⚠ and descend Chapel Hill

24 18.4 mi Turn right at T- junction into Kenwyn Street, proceed along City Road and Charles Street, and turn left at T- junction into Lemon Street
  18.5 mi Finish Lemon Quay/The Piazza Ⓟ ☕ 🚻 🚻 🏛 🚲 GR SW827447

TRURO - FALMOUTH

0.0 mi Start Lemon Quay/The Piazza Ⓟ 🚻 ☕ 🚻 🚲 GR SW827447
From The Piazza, follow one-way system into Lemon Street, take first right into Charles Street, City Road and Kenwyn Street

24 0.3 mi Fork left to climb Chapel Hill

23 0.7 mi Cross dual carriageway A390 Green Lane ⚠ and descend hill

22 1.8 mi Turn left and cross railway bridge

21 2.5 mi Straight on at crossroads

20 2.8 mi Straight on at crossroads

19 4.1 mi Turn right at T- junction

18 4.7 mi Turn right into visitor's area of Bissoe Cycle Hire Ⓟ 🚲 🚲 ☕ GR SW769415 Turn right out of visitor's centre and cross bridge over Carnon River

17 5.5 mi Turn left at T- junction in Cusgarne and proceed through Frogpool 🏛

16 6.1 mi Turn right at crossroads at top of hill

15 7.2 mi Turn left at crossroads with 'No Entry' straight ahead

14 7.3 mi Turn sharp right ⚠ on main Falmouth - Redruth road A393

13 7.4 mi Turn left

12 7.7 mi Turn left

11 9.0 mi Turn right at T- junction and cross bridge

10 9.3 mi Turn left at T-junction into Stithians ℗ 🚻 ☕ 🚹🚺 🏛 GR SW732369

9 9.7 mi Proceed through Stithians village and turn right at crossroads (🕇 Helston)

8 11.3 mi Turn left

7 11.8 mi Turn left ⚠ at T-junction onto main Falmouth - Helston road A394

6 11.9 mi Turn right ⚠ at Herniss (🕇 Halvasso) and pass cement works on left

5 13.9 mi Turn left (🕇 Penryn) and proceed through Treverva and Lamanva

4 15.5 mi Straight on at crossroads (🕇 Penryn) or turn left (🕇 Mabe) for
Argal Reservoir ℗ ☕ 🚹🚺 GR SW7623287

3 17.0 mi Turn right into Kergilliack Road (🕇 Falmouth)

2 17.2 mi Straight on at roundabout (🕇 Falmouth) into Trescobeas Road and then
Kimberley Park Road

1 18.1 mi Straight on at traffic lights down Kimberley Park Road and past Kimberley
Park on right, into Berkeley Vale and follow the one-way system into The Moor
18.5 mi Finish The Moor, Falmouth ℗ 🚹🚺 ☕ 🚻 🏛 🚲 GR SW806329

TRURO CATHEDRAL

PENDENNIS CASTLE

FALMOUTH

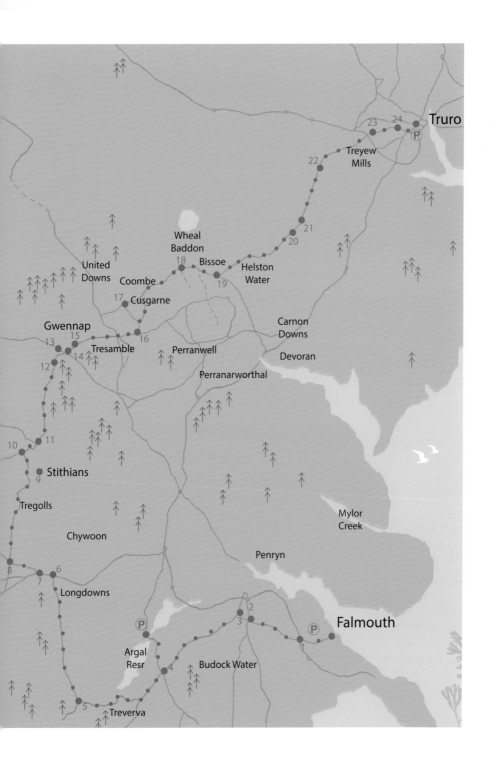

Truro

23 24

Treyew
Mills

22

21
20

Wheal
Baddon

18   Bissoe
United   Helston
Downs   Coombe   Water
17 Cusgarne   19

Gwennap   Carnon
13 15   Downs
       Tresamble
12 14   Devoran
                   Perranwell
            Perranarworthal

10   11

9   Stithians

Tregolls

Chywoon
                   Mylor
                   Creek

                   Penryn

8 6   Longdowns   2
7   3   Falmouth
                            1
Argal
Resr   4   Budock Water

5
Treverva

39

12 / ST AUSTELL - BODMIN

DISTANCE:	**14 miles**
TIME:	**2 hours 45 minutes** (at 5 mph), **1 hour 25 minutes** (at 10 mph), **55 minutes** (at 15 mph)
SURFACE:	Tarmac lanes and B roads
TERRAIN:	Hilly
BIKE:	Mountain, hybrid, cyclocross, road
PARKING:	Priory Road car park, St Austell PL25 5AB, Fore Street car park, Bodmin PL31 2DB
OPINION:	Once clear of the town, you will encounter little-used lanes winding through deepest Cornwall. Be prepared for some hills, although this ride has excellent refreshments and facilities at both the Eden Project and Lanhydrock House and Gardens. If you start and finish at the Eden Project and Lanhydrock House, you'll still see the best parts of the route, and miss out the busy urban roads and many of the hills. Apart from a short section around the Eden Project, the route follows the Sustrans National Cycle Route 3, so the distinctive blue signs may be used instead of the directions below.

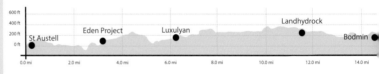

ST AUSTELL - BODMIN

0.0 mi Start St Austell Church Street Ⓟ 🚻 🚲 ☕ 🛍 🏛 GR SX013524
Leave via Market Street and Trevarthian Road (⌖ 3) and cycle past the railway station

1   0.2 mi At mini roundabout cycle straight on across railway bridge and continue along Carlyon Road, Polkyth Road, Sandy Hill, Bethel Road and Trenowah Road

2   1.9 mi At roundabout with A391 cycle straight on along Trenowah Road

3   2.2 mi At Tregrehan Mills crossroads straight on up steep hill

4   3.1 mi At crossroads turn left (⌖ Luxulyan) and pass Eden Project GR SX048547 on left

5   4.0 mi Turn right (⌖ 3)

6   4.6 mi Turn left (⌖ Luxulyan) and pass under railway bridge and viaduct

7 5.8 mi Turn left uphill (⼗ Luxulyan)

8 6.1 mi Luxulyan ℗ 🏛 GR SX052581 In village, turn right by church

9 6.3 mi At junction keep right

10 6.4 mi At junction keep right and soon pass quarry on right

11 7.9 mi At T- junction turn left (⼗ 3)

12 9.6 mi At Trebell Green road triangle turn right

13 10.2 mi At T- junction turn right (⼗ Bodmin)

14 11.7 mi At roundabout straight on joining cycle track parallel to road
(or turn right into Lanhydrock Estate ℗ 🍴 🚻 GR SX081638)

15 12.4 mi Cross bridge over A30 dual carriageway and bear right on cycle path

16 12.6 mi Turn left into lane

17 13.1 mi Turn left onto cycle/footpath and bear left downhill

18 13.3 mi At junction keep right into Island Lanes

19 13.4 mi At junction with B3268 turn right ⚠ and proceed straight on to town centre

14.5 mi Finish Bodmin ℗ 🚻 🚲 🍴 🏛 GR SX

LANHYDROCK

Dunmere

Bodmin

P

The
Beacon

Bodmin & Wenford Rly

19

17

18

16

15

Foxpark

14

13

12

Trebell
Green

Bokiddick
Downs

11

Tredinnick

10

9

Luxulyan

8

7

P

6

5

Eden
Project

St Blazey

Carvear
Moor

4

Tregrehan Mills

3

2

P

St Austell

Charlestown

BODMIN - ST AUSTELL

0.0 mi Start Bodmin ⓟ 👫 🚲 ☕ 🚻 🏛 GR SX072671 Leave along Fore Street, turn left uphill along Robartes Road, left into Beacon Road, cross railway bridge and turn right ⚠ to proceed along B3268

19 1.7 mi Fork left into Island Lanes

18 1.8 mi Turn left onto cycle/footpath

17 1.9 mi Keep right just before road and join lane turning right

16 2.4 mi Turn right onto cycle/footpath just before main A30 dual carriageway

15 2.6 mi Cross A30 dual carriageway on bridge and follow cycle/footpath parallel to road

14 3.3 mi Join road ⚠ and at roundabout take 2nd exit (or turn left into Lanhydrock Estate ⓟ ☕ 👫 GR SX081638)

13 4.8 mi At junction turn left (🍴 Trebell Green)

12 5.2 mi At Trebell Green road triangle turn left

11 6.9 mi At junction turn right (🍴 3)

10 8.4 mi At junction keep left

9 8.5 mi At junction keep left, and proceed into Luxulyan ⓟ 🚻 🏛 GR SX052581

8 8.8 mi At church in Luxulyan turn left

7 9.1 mi At bottom of hill turn right and proceed under viaduct and railway bridge

6 10.3 mi At junction turn right

5 10.9 mi Turn left and pass Eden Project GR SX048547 on right

4 11.8 mi At crossroads turn right and proceed down steep hill

3 12.7 mi At bottom of hill at Tregrehan Mills crossroads straight on

2 13.0 mi At roundabout with A391 straight on along Trenowah Road, Bethel Road, Sandy Hill, Polkyth Road and Carlyon Road

1 14.7 mi At mini roundabout turn left to join cycle route past railway station, and then turn left down Trevarthian Road

14.9 mi Finish St Austell Church Street ⓟ 👫 🚲 ☕ 🚻 🏛 GR SX013524

EDEN PROJECT

13 / **PERRANPORTH** - PORTREATH

DISTANCE: **12 miles**

TIME: **2 hours 25 minutes** (at 5 mph), **1 hour 10 minutes** (at 10 mph), **50 minutes** (at 15 mph)

SURFACE: Tarmac lanes and B roads

TERRAIN: Hilly

BIKE: Mountain, hybrid, cyclocross, road

PARKING: The Promenade car park, Perranporth TR6 0JN, The Beach car park, Portreath TR16 4NQ

OPINION: This hilly ride links two of Cornwall's iconic north coast surfing beaches and gives you the opportunity to visit Porthtowan and St Agnes if you like a few extra miles and hills.

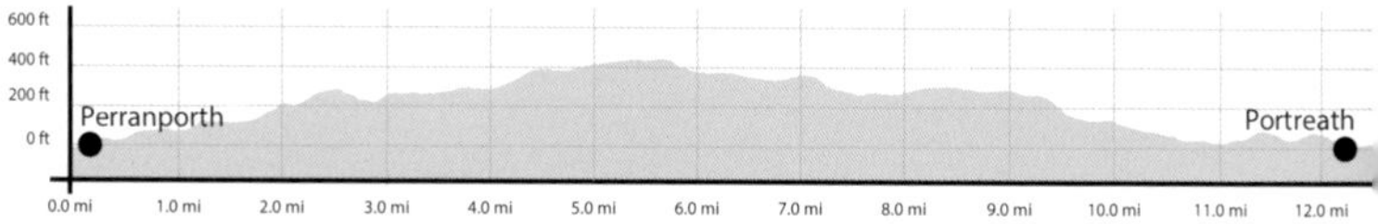

PERRANPORTH - PORTREATH

No. on maps

0.0 mi Start Perranporth GR SW756542 From the foot of Liskey Hill (B3284) take Boscawen Road, and proceed along Perrancoombe

1 1.0 mi Turn right when the road swings left uphill

2 1.7 mi Turn right at junction and proceed uphill

3 2.2 mi At top of hill turn left at T- junction onto B3285 (St Agnes)

4 2.7 mi Turn left on downhill bend (Truro)

5 3.1 mi Fork right immediately after crossing disused railway line

6 3.9 mi Turn left at T- junction (turn right to visit St Agnes)

7 4.4 mi Turn right at T- junction

8 5.1 mi Turn right at T- junction onto B3277 ⚠ (St Agnes), then immediately turn left (Skinner's Bottom)

9 5.2 mi Turn right (Skinner's Bottom)

10 5.4 mi Fork left (Blackwater)

11 5.8 mi Straight on at crossroads

12 7.1 mi Turn right at T- junction (Porthtowan)

13 7.3 mi Fork left (straight on to visit Porthtowan)

14 7.8 mi Turn right

15 8.7 mi Turn left at crossroads and at bottom of hill pass 🚲 on right
16 10.2 mi Turn right at T- junction onto B3300 (⍡ Portreath)
12.2 mi Finish Portreath Ⓟ ⁂ ☕ 🛏 🚲 🚲 GR SW653453

PORTREATH - PERRANPORTH

0.0 mi Start Portreath Ⓟ ⁂ ☕ 🛏 🚲 GR SW653453 Leave along Penberthy Road heading towards Redruth

16 2.0 mi Turn left (⍡ Porthtowan) and pass 🚲 on left
15 3.5 mi At top of hill turn right at crossroads (straight on to visit Porthtowan)
14 4.4 mi Turn left at T- junction
13 4.9 mi Turn right at junction
12 5.1 mi Turn left (⍡ Skinner's Bottom)
11 6.2 mi Straight on at crossroads
10 6.5 mi Turn right at junction
9 6.7 mi Turn left at T- junction
8 6.8 mi Turn right at T- junction onto B3277 ⚠ (⍡ Truro) then immediately turn left (⍡ Mithian)
7 7.5 mi Fork left
6 8.0 mi Fork right (straight on to visit St Agnes)
5 8.7 mi Turn left at junction
4 9.1 mi Turn right at T- junction onto B3235 (⍡ Perranporth)
3 9.6 mi Turn right (⍡ Perrancoombe)
2 10.1 mi Fork left at bottom of hill
1 10.8 mi Keep left at junction into Perrancoombe and proceed into Boscawen Road
12.2 mi Finish Perranporth Ⓟ ⁂ ☕ 🛏 🏛 GR SW756542

PORTREATH

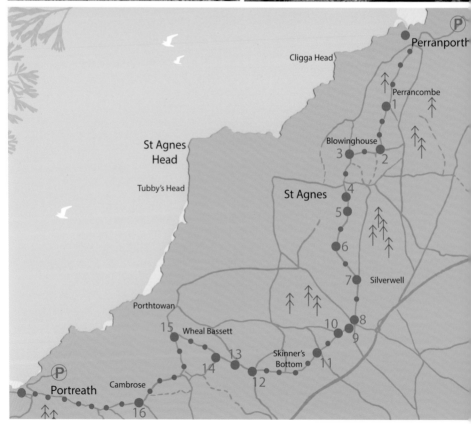

Perranporth

Cligga Head

Perrancombe

1

Blowinghouse

3   2

St Agnes
Head

4

Tubby's Head

St Agnes

5

6

Silverwell

7

Porthtowan

8

10

9

15   Wheal Bassett

13   Skinner's
Bottom

14   11

12

Cambrose

Portreath

16

14 / **PORTREATH** - HAYLE

DISTANCE:	**10 miles**
TIME:	**2 hours** (at 5 mph), **1 hour** (at 10 mph), **40 minutes** (at 15 mph)
SURFACE:	Mainly tarmac lanes and B roads
TERRAIN:	Undulating after initial steep climb out of Portreath
BIKE:	Mountain, hybrid, cyclocross, road
PARKING:	The Beach car park, Portreath TR16 4NQ, Foundry Square car park, Hayle TR27 4HQ
OPINION:	Once you have conquered the initial climb out of Portreath this is a great route if you like to enjoy spectacular views over St Ives Bay or if you wish to visit Tehidy Woods, Hell's Mouth, or Godrevy, Gwithian or Hayle beaches.

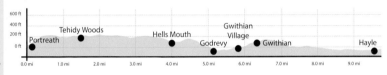

PORTREATH – HAYLE

No. on maps

0.0 mi Start Portreath Ⓟ 🚻 ☕ 🛍 🚲 GR SW653453 Leave by climbing Tregea Hill on the B3301

1 1.5 mi Pass entrance to Tehidy Woods Ⓟ 🚻 ☕ GR SW640437

2 4.0 mi Pass Hell's Mouth Ⓟ ☕ GR SW603428

3 5.2 mi Pass entrance to Godrevy Ⓟ 🚻 ☕ GR SW587420

4 5.8 mi Gwithian Village Ⓟ 🏛 GR SW585412

5 6.2 mi Pass entrance to Gwithian beach Ⓟ 🚻 ☕ GR SW580406

6 7.8 mi At mini roundabouts turn right

7 8.1 mi Turn right along Lethlean Lane

8 8.3 mi Turn left along Glebe Row

9 8.5 mi Turn left, then immediately right along King George V Memorial Walk

10 9.1 mi At T- junction turn left along North Quay

11 9.2 mi At T- junction ⚠ turn right onto main road to town centre

9.6 mi Finish Hayle Foundry Square Ⓟ 🚻 ☕ 🛍 🚲 🏛 GR SW558371

ROAD 14

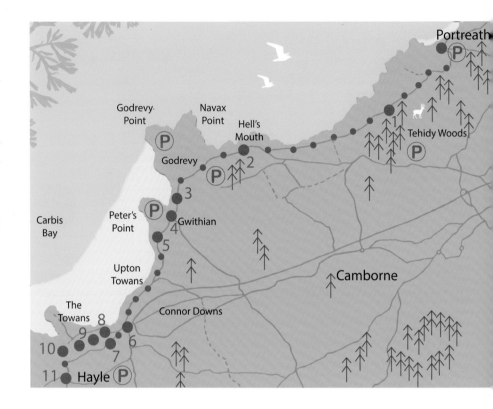

HAYLE - PORTREATH

0.0 mi Start Hayle Foundry Square ℗ 👫 ☕ 🛠 🏛 GR SW558371

Proceed along Penpol Terrace in Camborne direction

11 0.4 mi Turn left into North Quay

10 0.5 mi Turn right along King George V Memorial Walk

9 1.1 mi Turn left then immediately right into Glebe Row

8 1.3 mi Turn right along Lethlean Lane

7 1.5 mi Turn left onto main road ⚠

6 1.8 mi Turn left at mini roundabouts into Loggans Road B3301

5 3.4 mi Pass entrance to Gwithian beach ℗ 👫 ☕ GR SW580406

4 3.8 mi Gwithian Village ℗ 🏛 GR SW585412

3 4.4 mi Pass entrance to Godrevy ℗ 👫 ☕ GR SW587420

2 5.6 mi Pass Hell's Mouth ℗ ☕ GR SW603428

1 8.1 mi Pass entrance to Tehidy Woods ℗ 👫 ☕ GR SW640437

9.6 mi Finish Portreath ℗ 👫 ☕ 🛠 GR SW653453